"It's hard to connect with your child without first understanding where they are. As counselors and speakers at parenting events across the country, we spend a great deal of time teaching parents about development. To know *where* your child is—not just physically, but emotionally, socially, and spiritually, helps you to truly know and understand *who* your child is. And that understanding is the key to connecting. The Phase Guides give you the tools to do just that. Our wise friends Reggie and Kristen have put together an insightful, hopeful, practical, and literal year-by-year guide that will help you to understand and connect with your child at every age."

SISSY GOFF
M.ED., LPC-MHSP, DIRECTOR OF CHILD & ADOLESCENT COUNSELING AT DAYSTAR COUNSELING MINISTRIES IN NASHVILLE, TENNESSEE, SPEAKER AND AUTHOR OF ARE MY KIDS ON TRACK?

"These resources for parents are fantastically empowering, absolute in th simplicity, and completely doable in every way. The hard work that has g into the Phase Project will echo through the next generation of children powerful ways."

JENNIFER WALKER
RN BSN, AUTHOR AND FOUNDER OF MOMS ON CALL

"We all know where we want to end up in our parenting, but how to ge can seem like an unsolved mystery. Through the Phase Project series, F Joiner and Kristen Ivy team up to help us out. The result is a resource t us through the different seasons of raising children, and provides a roa parenting in such a way that we finish up with very few regrets."

SANDRA STANLEY
FOSTER CARE ADVOCATE, BLOGGER, WIFE TO ANDY STANLEY, MOTHER OF THREE

"Not only are the Phase Guides the most creative and well-thought-out guides to parenting I have ever encountered, these books are ESSENTIAL to my daily parenting. With a 13-year-old, 11-year-old, and 9-year-old at home, I am swimming in their wake of daily drama and delicacy. These books are a reminder to enjoy every second. Because it's just a phase."

CARLOS WHITTAKER
AUTHOR, SPEAKER, FATHER OF THREE

"As the founder of Minnie's Food Pantry, I see thousands of people each month with children who will benefit from the advice, guidance, and nuggets of information on how to celebrate and understand the phases of their child's life. Too often we feel like we're losing our mind when sweet little Johnny starts to change his behavior into a person we do not know. I can't wait to start implementing the principles of these books with my clients to remind them . . . it's just a phase."

CHERYL JACKSON
FOUNDER OF MINNIE'S FOOD PANTRY, AWARD-WINNING PHILANTHROPIST, AND GRANDMOTHER

"I began exploring this resource with my counselor hat on, thinking how valuable this will be for the many parents I spend time with in my office. I ended up taking my counselor hat off and putting on my parent hat. Then I kept thinking about friends who are teachers, coaches, youth pastors, and children's ministers, who would want this in their hands. What a valuable resource the Orange team has given us to better understand and care for the kids and adolescents we love. I look forward to sharing it broadly."

DAVID THOMAS
LMSW, DIRECTOR OF FAMILY COUNSELING, DAYSTAR COUNSELING MINISTRIES, SPEAKER AND AUTHOR OF ARE MY KIDS ON TRACK? *AND* WILD THINGS: THE ART OF NURTURING BOYS

"I have always wished someone would hand me a manual for parenting. Well, the Phase Guides are more than what I wished for. They guide, inspire, and challenge me as a parent—while giving me incredible insight into my children at each age and phase. Our family will be using these every year!"

COURTNEY DEFEO
AUTHOR OF IN THIS HOUSE, WE WILL GIGGLE, *MOTHER OF TWO*

"As I speak to high school students and their parents, I always wonder to myself: What would it have been like if they had better seen what was coming next? What if they had a guide that would tell them what to expect and how to be ready? What if they could anticipate what is predictable about the high school years before they actually hit? These Phase Guides give a parent that kind of preparation so they can have a plan when they need it most."

JOSH SHIPP
AUTHOR, TEEN EXPERT, AND YOUTH SPEAKER

"The Phase Guides are incredibly creative, well researched, and filled with inspirational actions for everyday life. Each age-specific guide is catalytic for equipping parents to lead and love their kids as they grow up. I'm blown away and deeply encouraged by the content and by its creators. I highly recommend Phase resources for all parents, teachers, and influencers of children. This is the stuff that challenges us and changes our world. Get them. Read them. And use them!"

DANIELLE STRICKLAND
OFFICER WITH THE SALVATION ARMY, AUTHOR, SPEAKER, MOTHER OF TWO

"It's true that parenting is one of life's greatest joys but it is not without its challenges. If we're honest, parenting can sometimes feel like trying to choreograph a dance to an ever-changing beat. It can be clumsy and riddled with well-meaning missteps. If parenting is a dance, this Parenting Guide is a skilled instructor refining your technique and helping you move gracefully to a steady beat. For those of us who love to plan ahead, this guide will help you anticipate what's to come so you can be poised and ready to embrace the moments you want to enjoy."

TINA NAIDOO
MSSW, LCSW EXECUTIVE DIRECTOR, THE POTTER'S HOUSE OF DALLAS, INC.

PARENTING YOUR NINTH GRADER

A GUIDE TO MAKING THE MOST OF THE "THIS IS ME NOW" PHASE

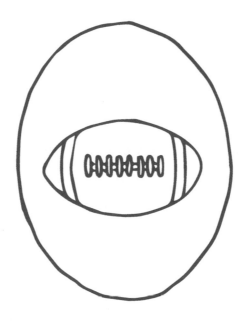

KRISTEN IVY AND REGGIE JOINER

PARENTING YOUR NINTH GRADER
A GUIDE TO MAKING THE MOST OF THE
"THIS IS ME NOW" PHASE

Published by Orange, a division of The reThink Group, Inc.,
5870 Charlotte Lane, Suite 300,
Cumming, GA 30040 U.S.A.

All Scripture quotations, unless otherwise indicated, are taken from the Holy
Bible, New International Version®, NIV®. Copyright ©1973, 1978, 1984, 2011 by
Biblica, Inc.™ Used by permission of Zondervan. All rights reserved worldwide.
www.zondervan.com The "NIV" and "New International Version" are trademarks
registered in the United States Patent and Trademark Office by Biblica, Inc.™

©2017 The Phase Project
Authors: Kristen Ivy and Reggie Joiner
Lead Editor: Karen Wilson
Editing Team: Melanie Williams, Hannah Crosby, Sherry Surratt

Art Direction: Ryan Boon and Hannah Crosby
Book Design: FiveStone and Sharon van Rossum
Project Manager : Nate Brandt

Printed in the United States of America
First Edition 2017
12 13 14 15 16 17 18 19 20 21

02/2020

Special thanks to:

Jim Burns, Ph.D for guidance and consultation on having conversations about sexual integrity

Jon Acuff for guidance and consultation on having conversations about technological responsibility

Jean Sumner, MD for guidance and consultation on having conversations about healthy habits

Every educator, counselor, community leader, and researcher who invested in the Phase Project

TABLE OF CONTENTS

HOW TO USE THIS ~~BOOK~~ ~~JOURNAL~~ GUIDE

The guide you hold in your hand doesn't have very many words, but it does have a lot of ideas. Some of these ideas come from thousands of hours of research. Others come from parents, educators, and volunteers who spend every day with kids the same age as yours. This guide won't tell you everything about your kid, but it will tell you a few things about kids at this age.

The best way to use this guide is to take what these pages tell you about ninth graders and combine it with what you know is true about *your* ninth grader.

Let's sum it up:

THINGS ABOUT NINTH GRADERS +
THOUGHTS ABOUT *YOUR* NINTH GRADER =
YOUR GUIDE TO THE NEXT 52 WEEKS OF PARENTING

After each idea in this guide, there are pages with a few questions designed to prompt you to think about your kid, your family, and yourself as a parent. The only guarantee we give to parents who use this guide is this: You will mess up some things as a parent this year. Actually, that's a guarantee to every parent, regardless. But you, you picked up this book! You want to be a better parent. And that's what we hope this guide will do: help you parent your ninth grader just a little better, simply because you paused to consider a few ideas that can help you make the most of this phase.

THE NINTH GRADE PHASE

Ninth grade is a year of awakening. It's like the moment when . . .
Peter Parker discovers his amazing spider powers.
Katniss Everdeen realizes her unique strength and talent.
Batman takes Robin under his wing and trains him how to
fight crime.

Ninth grade is the year our kids truly begin to discover who they
are and embark on journeys of unimagined power.

For me, ninth grade couldn't have come soon enough. In eighth
grade, I got kicked off my basketball team because I'd forged the
signature on my health physical. I got a D in math and Cs in other
classes. In the middle of the year, my family moved to a low-
income neighborhood, and I had to navigate a new school.

Four years later, as a senior, I was an all-state athlete and in the
top one percent of my class. I was accepted by every college I
applied to—including Harvard and Yale—and I had confidence that
I'd never imagined possible in middle school.

There was something about ninth grade that forever changed the
trajectory of my future. I realize my experience is unique, but it
points to the potential of this phase to change a person's story and
launch them into adulthood.

Sure, ninth grade doesn't come without challenges. There are new
academic pressures, the hormones of puberty are still running
high, and the opportunity to participate in unhealthy activities

has never been greater. But don't let that overshadow the unprecedented possibilities.

Teenagers in this phase begin to self-reflect in ways that weren't possible in middle school. In my ninth grade year, a mentor gave me a journal where I could write about the things that mattered to me. I didn't just write about girls, my classes, or sports. I wrote about my faith. My goals. My dreams. Ninth grade changed me because someone empowered me to discover who I really was.

Taking time to reflect didn't mean my problems went away. My family still lived in low-income housing all throughout high school. My father was legally blind and didn't work. My mother made less than $10 an hour. And my best friend, my brother Tewolde, was killed by a drunk driver my sophomore year.

But those challenges didn't detract from what was happening in me as I became aware of who I was made to be. That's why I've spent the last fifteen years speaking to over a million students. I'm always looking for that moment of awakening. That moment when a kid realizes they can be and do more than they ever thought.

That's the challenge I would give to every parent. Rediscover your ninth grader with fresh eyes, and empower them to rediscover who they are. Don't allow yourself to buy into the myth that high school students are lazy, uninspired, or self-absorbed. Nothing could be further from the truth.

Ninth graders are superheroes, ready to give and grow in incredible ways.

- MAWI ASGEDOM
CEO OF MAWI LEARNING, AUTHOR, SPEAKER, & EDUCATOR

52 WEEKS

—

TO PARENT YOUR

NINTH GRADER

WHEN YOU SEE
HOW MUCH

Time

YOU HAVE LEFT

—

YOU TEND TO DO

More

WITH THE TIME
YOU HAVE NOW.

THERE ARE APPROXIMATELY
936 WEEKS
FROM THE TIME A BABY IS BORN UNTIL THEY GROW UP AND MOVE TO WHATEVER IS NEXT.

On the day your kid starts ninth grade, you have 208 weeks remaining. Just to put that in perspective, your ninth grader is probably something like 724 weeks old! These are the final weeks. Get ready. The next 208 weeks will move faster than all the others.

Every week counts, but each week might not feel significant. There may be weeks this year when all you feel like you accomplished was remembering which subjects they are taking. That's okay.

Take a deep breath.
You don't have to get everything done this week.

But what happens in your teenager's life week after week—for the next four years—adds up. So, it might be a good idea to put a number to your weeks.

MEASURE IT OUT.

Write down the number of weeks you have left with your ninth grader before they potentially graduate high school.

HINT: If you want a little help counting it out, you can download the free Parent Cue app on all mobile platforms.

_____

_____

_____

_____

CREATE A VISUAL COUNTDOWN.

Find a jar and fill it with one marble for each week you have remaining with your ninth grader. Then remove one marble every week as a reminder to make the most of your time.

Where can you place your visual countdown so you will see it frequently?

_____

_____

_____

_____

_____

Which day of the week is best for you to remove a marble?

_____

_____

_____

Is there anything you want to do each week as you remove a marble? *(Examples: say a prayer, send an encouraging text, retell one favorite memory from this past week)*

_____

_____

_____

_____

_____

_____

_____

_____

_____

_____

_____

_____

_____

EVERY PHASE IS A

TIMEFRAME

IN A KID'S LIFE

WHEN YOU CAN

LEVERAGE

DISTINCTIVE

OPPORTUNITIES

TO INFLUENCE

THEIR

future.

YOU ONLY HAVE
52 WEEKS
WITH YOUR NINTH GRADER

while they are still in ninth grade.
Then they will be in tenth grade,
and you will never know them as a ninth grader again.

Or, to say it another way:
Before you know it, your teenager will . . .
discover a new club or activity.
quit a sport you thought they loved.
talk to online friends you've never met.

That's not intended to stress you out. (*Although it might do that, too.*)
It's to remind you of the potential of this phase.

Before ninth grade is finished, there are some distinctive opportunities you don't want to miss. So, as you count down the next 52 weeks with your ninth grader, pay attention to what makes these weeks uniquely different from the time you've already spent together and the weeks you will have when they move to the next phase.

Time travel for a minute. Remember what it was like to be in ninth grade. What are the best things your parents did for you during that phase of your life? What do you want to try to do differently than your parents?

_____

_____

_____

_____

_____

_____

_____

_____

_____

_____

_____

_____

_____

_____

_____

_____

What do you think is going to be different about your ninth grader's freshman year than your freshman year?

_____

_____

_____

_____

_____

_____

_____

_____

_____

_____

_____

_____

_____

_____

_____

_____

_____

_____

_____

_____

What are some things you have noticed about your ninth grader in this phase that you really enjoy?

_____

_____

_____

_____

_____

_____

_____

_____

_____

_____

_____

_____

_____

_____

_____

_____

_____

_____

_____

What is something new you're learning as a parent during this phase?

_____

_____

_____

_____

_____

_____

_____

_____

_____

_____

_____

_____

_____

_____

_____

_____

_____

_____

NINTH GRADE

—

THE PHASE WHEN FRIENDSHIPS SHIFT, GRADES COUNT, AND INTERESTS CHANGE SO OFTEN YOUR TEENAGER HAS TO EXPLAIN,

"This is me now."

YOU MAY NOTICE A FEW NEW FRIENDS.

The average high school has 750 teenagers, 250 dating couples, and more than 50 options for extracurricular activities. With so many opportunities to connect, your high schooler may find their place in engineering class or on the debate team, in drama club or on the basketball court, in YMCA or Beta Club.

THERE IS A NEW ACADEMIC REALITY.

Ninth grade means increased demands for personal responsibility. For those headed to college, grades begin to count toward future admission. For everyone, grades count toward a high school diploma.

THIS IS A YEAR OF IDENTIFYING TALENTS.

By the end of this year, your teenager will have a more stable sense of who they are. Frankly, they may be a little frustrated you haven't known who they were all along. (Why not? It's been so obvious.) Listen carefully. Pay attention. Stalk them openly. The greatest thing you can do in this phase is to continually rediscover who they are becoming and know where they are finding acceptance.

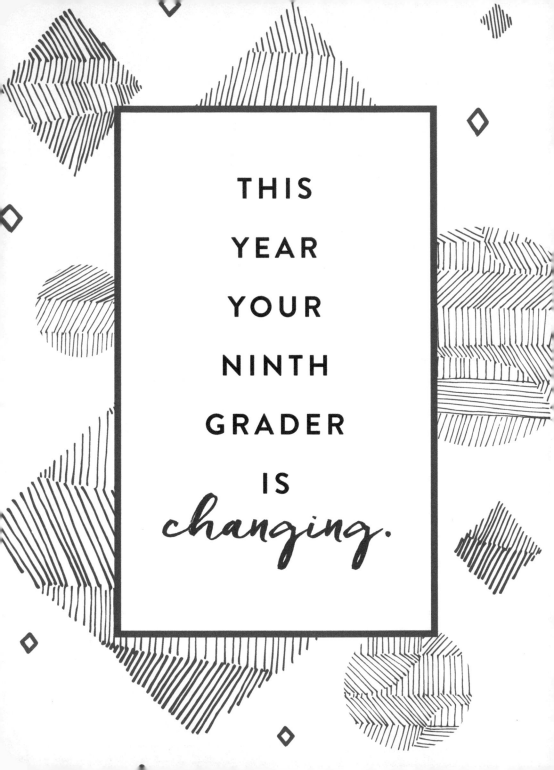

THIS

YEAR

YOUR

NINTH

GRADER

IS

changing.

PHYSICALLY

- Has difficulty falling asleep before 11pm, but still needs 9 hours of sleep per day

- Guys are getting taller, smellier, hairier, and gaining muscle mass; may also experience voice changes, weird dreams, and increased acne

- Girls bodies take on an adult physical appearance; after menstruation, increase in height will slow and then stop

MENTALLY

- Increasingly able to focus, recall, and organize information

- Overly self-aware; may think, "Everybody's watching me."

- Wired for risk-taking and sensational experiences

- Resists potentially embarrassing situations

- "I'm bored" often means, "I don't understand"

SOCIALLY

- Girls begin wearing make-up on a regular basis

- Increased interest in sexual expression, but dating tends to be short-lived

- Say they want parents to listen more than advise

- May be tempted to change their appearance or behavior to gain acceptance

EMOTIONALLY

- Feels empowered through choices rather than rules

- May still feel insecure about their changing body

- May experience changes in motivation

- Seeks experiences that create intense feelings and emotions

- Increasingly vulnerable to addiction, such as self-harm, alcohol, and pornography

What are some changes you are noticing in your ninth grader?

_____

_____

_____

_____

_____

_____

_____

You may disagree with some of the characteristics we've shared about ninth graders. That's because every ninth grader is unique. What makes your ninth grader different from ninth graders in general?

_____

_____

_____

_____

_____

_____

_____

What impresses you about your ninth grader?

Mark this page. Some weeks it may be easy to focus only on what your ninth grader does wrong, so try to catch them doing something right. Write it down here. If you want to be really thorough, there are about 52 blank lines.

_____

_____

_____

_____

_____

_____

_____

_____

_____

_____

_____

_____

_____

_____

_____

_____

_____

_____

_____

_____

_____

_____

_____

_____

_____

_____

_____

_____

_____

_____

_____

_____

_____

_____

_____

_____

_____

_____

_____

_____

_____

_____

_____

_____

_____

_____

_____

_____

_____

_____

_____

_____

_____

_____

_____

YOUR KID NEEDS **6** THINGS OVER TIME

LOVE

WORDS

WORK

TRIBES

STORIES

FUN

OVER THE NEXT 208 WEEKS, YOUR NINTH GRADER WILL NEED MANY THINGS:

Some of the things your teenager needs will change over the next 208 weeks, but there are six things every kid needs at every phase. In fact, these things may be the most important things you give your high schooler (even more important than money—but they will probably ask you for money more often).

EVERY KID, AT EVERY PHASE, NEEDS . . .

♡ LOVE
to give them a sense of WORTH.

📖 STORIES
to give them a bigger PERSPECTIVE.

🏋 WORK
to give them SIGNIFICANCE.

♟ FUN
to give them CONNECTION.

👥 TRIBES
to give them BELONGING.

💬 WORDS
to give them DIRECTION.

The next few pages are designed to help you think about how you will give your teenager these six things, right now—while they are in ninth grade.

EVERY KID

NEEDS

love

OVER TIME

—

TO GIVE THEM

A SENSE OF

worth.

ONE QUESTION YOUR NINTH GRADER IS ASKING

High school means higher stakes. Many freshmen spend this year redefining who they thought they were or what they thought their future would be.

Your ninth grader is asking one major question:

"WHERE DO I BELONG?"

The friends your ninth grader makes in the first weeks of high school may determine the direction of their next four years. The adult mentors who show up weekly in your ninth grader's life may influence their perspective, decisions, and values. In order to give your ninth grader love, you need to do one thing:

MOBILIZE their potential.

Your ninth grader will feel most loved when they find acceptance in a group of peers and adult mentors. So, mobilize their potential to find acceptance by . . .

driving them where they need to go,

inviting new friends to your home,

or helping your ninth grader discover new places to plug in.

Mobilizing your freshman's potential requires paying attention to who they like spending time with. Who are your ninth grader's closest friends?

_____

_____

_____

_____

_____

_____

_____

_____

_____

_____

_____

_____

_____

_____

_____

_____

_____

What activities does your ninth grader seem to enjoy the most right now? *(If you don't know, it's okay to ask them.)*

HINT: Sometimes you can leverage the activities that interest your ninth grader to help them connect with new friends.

_____

_____

_____

_____

_____

_____

_____

_____

_____

_____

_____

_____

_____

_____

_____

_____

_____

How can you support your ninth grader's relationships so they have quality experiences with the right kind of people?

_____

_____

_____

_____

_____

_____

_____

_____

_____

_____

_____

_____

_____

_____

_____

_____

_____

_____

_____

_____

_____

As you know, parenting a teenager can be tough. It's impossible to love anyone with the effort a ninth grader requires if you are running on empty. What can you do to refuel each week so you are able to give your ninth grader the love they need?

_____

_____

_____

_____

_____

_____

_____

_____

_____

_____

_____

_____

_____

_____

_____

_____

_____

_____

_____

EVERY KID

NEEDS

stories

OVER TIME

—

TO GIVE THEM

A BIGGER

perspective.

BOOKS YOUR NINTH GRADER MIGHT BE READING

THE HITCHHIKER'S GUIDE TO THE GALAXY
by Douglas Adams

THE SISTERHOOD OF THE TRAVELING PANTS
by Ann Brashares

THE AWAKENING
by Kate Chopin

GREAT EXPECTATIONS
by Charles Dickens

ALAS, BABYLON
by Pat Frank

THE CURIOUS INCIDENT OF THE DOG IN THE NIGHT-TIME
by Mark Haddon

CATCH-22
by Joseph Heller

THE ILIAD / THE ODYSSEY
by Homer

THEIR EYES WERE WATCHING GOD
by Zora Neale Hurston

BRAVE NEW WORLD
by Aldous Huxley

ONE FLEW OVER THE CUCKOO'S NEST
by Ken Kesey

THE POISONWOOD BIBLE
by Barbara Kingsolver

TO KILL A MOCKINGBIRD
by Harper Lee

ANIMAL FARM
by George Orwell

ANTHEM
by Ayn Rand

ROMEO AND JULIET
by Shakespeare

FRANKENSTEIN
by Mary Shelley

THE HELP
by Kathryn Stockett

NIGHT
by Elie Wiesel

Share a story. Whether it's a book, play, TV series, or movie, what are some stories that engage your freshman?

_____

_____

_____

_____

_____

_____

_____

_____

_____

_____

_____

_____

_____

_____

_____

_____

_____

_____

What might happen to your relationship when you watch or read the same story together?

_____

_____

_____

_____

_____

_____

_____

_____

_____

_____

_____

_____

_____

_____

_____

_____

_____

_____

_____

Tell a story. As you watch your ninth grader live out their story, how can you act like a narrator to help them interpret who they are and what's happening? *(Example: "I wonder if your teammate walked away from you because they felt intimidated.")*

_____

_____

_____

_____

_____

_____

_____

_____

_____

_____

_____

_____

_____

_____

_____

_____

_____

Live a story. When a ninth grader serves others, they broaden their perspective by learning about someone else's story. Is there somewhere your ninth grader would enjoy serving on a regular basis?

_____

_____

_____

_____

_____

_____

_____

_____

_____

_____

_____

_____

_____

_____

_____

_____

EVERY KID

NEEDS

work

OVER TIME

—

TO GIVE

THEM

significance.

WORK YOUR
NINTH GRADER CAN DO

DO HOMEWORK

KEEP A PERSONAL
CALENDAR

MOW LAWNS
(yours or someone else's)

BABYSIT

TAKE OUT THE TRASH
OR RECYCLING

PREPARE A FAMILY MEAL

SORT, WASH, FOLD, IRON
AND PUT AWAY LAUNDRY

OPEN A
SAVINGS ACCOUNT

CHANGE BATTERIES IN A
SMOKE DETECTOR

USE A JIGSAW
WITH ASSISTANCE

PRACTICE A SPORT,
MUSICAL INSTRUMENT,
ART, OR OTHER SKILL

What are some ways your ninth grader already shows responsibility at home, at school, and in-between?

_____

_____

_____

_____

_____

_____

_____

_____

_____

_____

_____

_____

_____

_____

_____

_____

_____

_____

_____

How can you collaborate with your ninth grader to agree on which of their responsibilities matter most for your family and their future?

_____

_____

_____

_____

_____

_____

_____

_____

_____

_____

_____

_____

_____

_____

_____

_____

_____

_____

_____

Some days might be easier than others to motivate your ninth grader. What are some strategies you could employ to keep your ninth grader motivated?

_____

_____

_____

_____

_____

_____

_____

_____

_____

_____

_____

_____

_____

_____

_____

_____

_____

_____

What are things you (and your ninth grader) hope they will be able to do independently next year? How are you helping them develop those skills now?

_____

_____

_____

_____

_____

_____

_____

_____

_____

_____

_____

_____

_____

_____

_____

_____

_____

_____

_____

EVERY KID

NEEDS

fun

OVER TIME

—

TO GIVE

THEM

connection.

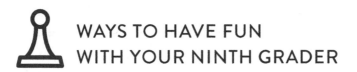

WAYS TO HAVE FUN WITH YOUR NINTH GRADER

WATCH A MOVIE

ATTEND A SPORTING EVENT

GO TO A CONCERT

WORK OUT TOGETHER

PLAY MUSIC TOGETHER

BUILD SOMETHING

COOK SOMETHING

GO ON A RUN

GO ON A HIKE

GO SHOPPING

SHOOT SOME HOOPS

WORK ON CAR REPAIRS

GET A MANICURE

WATCH A TV SERIES

GO TO A PLAY

GO FISHING

GO BOWLING

PLAY LASER TAG

HAVE A RESTAURANT THAT'S "YOURS"

TRY A NEW RESTAURANT OR FOOD TRUCK

PLANT A GARDEN

PLAY A BOARD GAME

PLAY A VIDEO GAME

PLAY CARDS

PLAY A GAME ON A PHONE APP

LAUNCH ROCKETS

LEARN TO DANCE

GO TO THE LAKE

RIDE A ROLLER COASTER

GO OUT FOR COFFEE

GO OUT FOR ICE CREAM

GO SEE A COMEDIAN

Whatever you do together for fun, try to offer suggestions based on what they enjoy—even at the expense of what you might enjoy a little more.

What are some activities your ninth grader enjoys that you could do as a family *(and maybe sometimes include their friends)*?

_____

_____

_____

_____

_____

_____

_____

_____

_____

_____

_____

_____

_____

_____

_____

_____

_____

_____

What are some activities your ninth grader enjoys that you could occasionally do together, one-on-one?

_____

_____

_____

_____

_____

_____

_____

_____

_____

When are the best times of the day, or week, for you to set aside to just have fun with your ninth grader?

_____

_____

_____

_____

_____

_____

Some days are *extra* fun days. What are some ways you want to celebrate the special days coming up this year?

NEXT BIRTHDAY

_____

_____

_____

_____

_____

_____

_____

_____

_____

_____

_____

_____

_____

_____

_____

_____

_____

HOLIDAYS

Consider celebrating a few random holidays: the first/last day of school, National Donut Day, Hamburger Month, Pajama Day.

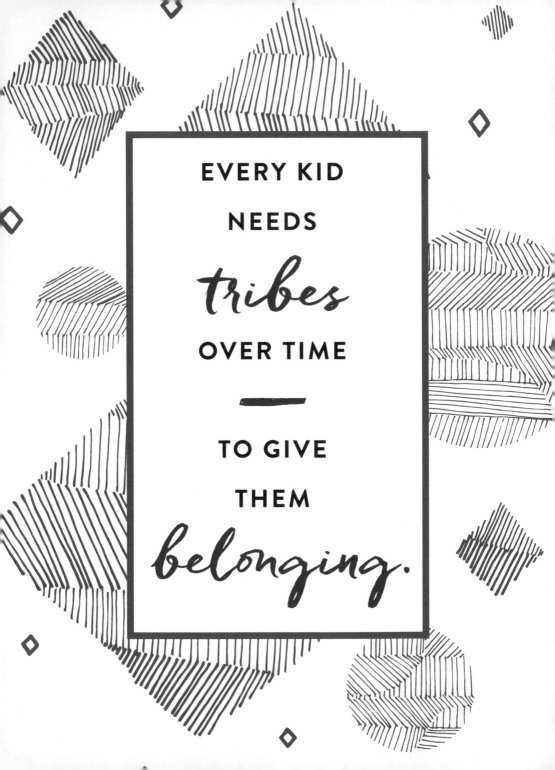

ADULTS WHO MIGHT INFLUENCE YOUR NINTH GRADER

PARENTS

COMMUNITY LEADERS

CHURCH LEADERS

GRANDPARENTS

FRIENDS' PARENTS

COACHES

CLUB SPONSORS

HIGH SCHOOL TEACHERS

TUTORS

You already know that friends matter to your ninth grader, but it can be easy to forget that ninth graders also need other adults in their tribe. List at least five adults who have the potential to positively influence your ninth grader.

_____

_____

_____

_____

_____

_____

_____

_____

_____

_____

_____

_____

_____

_____

_____

_____

_____

What would be good information for these people to know if they want to help or support your ninth grader this year?

_____

_____

_____

_____

_____

_____

_____

_____

_____

_____

_____

_____

_____

_____

_____

_____

_____

_____

_____

What are some upcoming events in your ninth grader's life that you could invite one or more of these adults to attend?

_____

_____

_____

_____

_____

_____

_____

_____

_____

_____

_____

_____

_____

_____

_____

_____

_____

_____

What are a few ways you could show these adults appreciation for the significant role they play in your kid's life?

_____

_____

_____

_____

_____

_____

_____

_____

_____

_____

_____

_____

_____

_____

_____

_____

_____

_____

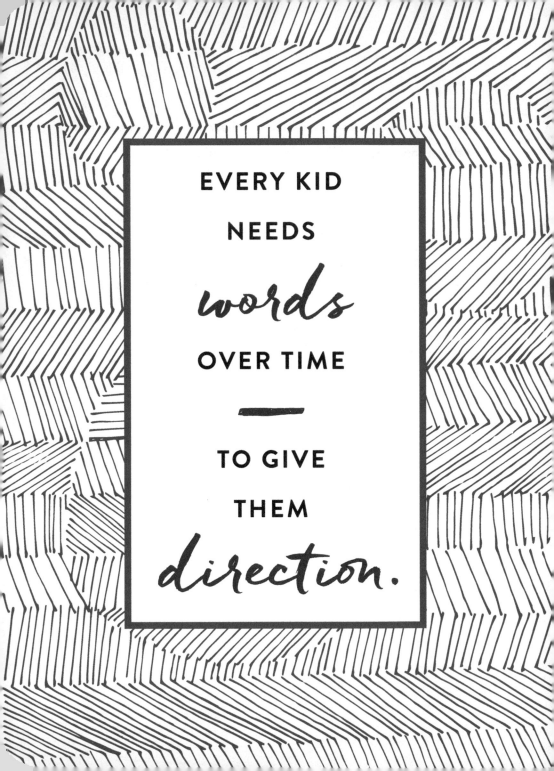

EVERY KID

NEEDS

words

OVER TIME

—

TO GIVE

THEM

direction.

WORDS YOUR NINTH GRADER NEEDS TO HEAR

GOOD MORNING!

I LOVE YOU

TELL ME MORE

HOW CAN I HELP?

WHAT DO YOU THINK?

I'M SORRY

I'M REALLY PROUD WHEN . . .

ME TOO

YOU ARE STARTING TO . . .

WANT A HUG?

YOU ARE BEAUTIFUL / HANDSOME

GOOD NIGHT!

THANK YOU FOR SPENDING TIME WITH US.

I LIKE YOU

WHEN YOU'RE WITH YOUR FRIENDS . . .

What are some ways you can share personal and specific encouragement with your ninth grader?

🔒 Hint: You might start with the things that impress you about your ninth grader from page 29.

_____

_____

_____

_____

_____

_____

_____

_____

_____

_____

_____

_____

_____

_____

_____

_____

_____

You might be impressed by the words that inspire your ninth grader. How might you encourage your ninth grader to share a quote, song lyric, Scripture, or thought that inspired them?

_____

_____

_____

_____

_____

_____

_____

_____

_____

_____

_____

_____

_____

_____

_____

_____

_____

_____

What are some quotes, lyrics, Scriptures, or inspirational thoughts you want to share with your ninth grader? Make it a habit to regularly text or send encouraging thoughts their way.

_____

_____

_____

_____

_____

_____

_____

_____

_____

_____

_____

_____

_____

_____

_____

_____

_____

FOUR CONVERSATIONS

—

TO HAVE IN THIS PHASE

WHEN YOU KNOW
WHERE YOU WANT
TO GO,

AND YOU KNOW
WHERE YOU ARE
NOW,

YOU CAN ALWAYS
DO SOMETHING

TO MOVE IN A
BETTER DIRECTION.

OVER THE NEXT 208 WEEKS, IT MAY BE HARD TO FIND TIME FOR CONVERSATIONS. WHEN YOU *DO* GET A FEW MINUTES TO TALK, IT CAN BE HARD TO KNOW WHAT TO SAY FIRST.

You want to talk about grades.

They want to ask about weekend plans.

But, in the middle of everything that's urgent, don't forget to have a few important conversations along the way as well.

WHAT YOU SAY ABOUT . . .
Health
Sex
Technology
or Faith

MAY IMPACT YOUR NINTH GRADER'S FUTURE EVEN MORE THAN BIOLOGY MIDTERMS.

The next pages are about the conversations that matter most. On the left page is a destination—what you might want to be true in your kid's life 208 weeks from now. On the right page is a goal for conversations with your ninth grader this year, and a few suggestions about what you might want to say.

Healthy habits

—

LEARNING TO STRENGTHEN MY BODY THROUGH EXERCISE, NUTRITION, AND SELF-ADVOCACY

THIS YEAR YOU WILL
ENCOURAGE A HEALTHY LIFESTYLE
SO THEY WILL SHARPEN THEIR PERSONAL AWARENESS
AND BALANCE DIET AND EXERCISE.

Maintain a good relationship with your pediatrician, and schedule a physical at least once per year. You can also encourage your ninth grader to develop healthy habits with a few simple words.

SAY THINGS LIKE . . .

"SOMETIMES YOU HAVE TO PAUSE TO SEE IF YOU ARE FEELING HUNGRY, THIRSTY, TIRED, OR ANXIOUS."

"WOULD YOU BE INTERESTED IN SEEING A COUNSELOR TO TALK ABOUT THAT?"
(Teenagers often need counseling for emotional support and coaching.)

"GOD MADE MY BODY THE WAY IT IS. AND, I'VE LEARNED TO LIKE HOW I LOOK."

"WHEN WAS THE LAST TIME YOU DRANK SOME WATER?"
(Ninth graders sometimes forget to stay hydrated.)

WILL YOU SHOOT SOME HOOPS WITH ME?
(Stay active together.)

"YOU CAN'T BE IN MARCHING BAND AND THE SCHOOL PLAY AT THE SAME TIME."
(Help them set reasonable expectations for activities and sports.)

"YOU CAN'T REPLACE SLEEP WITH ENERGY DRINKS."
(Caution excessive caffeine and monitor bedtimes—including cell phone use after bedtime.)

What are some activities you can do with your ninth grader that require a little bit of exercise?

_____

_____

_____

_____

_____

_____

_____

_____

_____

_____

_____

_____

_____

_____

_____

_____

_____

_____

_____

Freshmen can be sensitive about their bodies. What's one way you can promote a healthy body image for your ninth grader?

_____

_____

_____

_____

_____

_____

_____

_____

_____

_____

_____

_____

_____

_____

_____

_____

_____

_____

_____

_____

_____

Do you have any specific concerns when it comes to your ninth grader's physical or mental health? Who will help you monitor and improve their health this year?

_____

_____

_____

_____

_____

_____

_____

_____

_____

_____

_____

_____

_____

_____

_____

_____

_____

What are your own health goals for this year? How can you improve the habits in your own life?

_____

_____

_____

_____

_____

_____

_____

_____

_____

_____

_____

_____

_____

_____

_____

_____

_____

_____

Sexual integrity

—

GUARDING MY

POTENTIAL FOR

INTIMACY THROUGH

APPROPRIATE

BOUNDARIES

AND MUTUAL

RESPECT

THIS YEAR YOU WILL
COACH THEM TOWARD HEALTHY RELATIONSHIPS
SO THEY WILL ESTABLISH PERSONAL BOUNDARIES AND PRACTICE MUTUAL RESPECT.

Over 70% of high schoolers say they have dated, and 30% of ninth graders report being sexually active. So, regardless of your ninth grader's relationship status, your conversations about sex and dating will become much less theoretical in this phase and the phases to come.

SAY THINGS LIKE . . .

"THANK YOU FOR TALKING ABOUT THIS. CAN WE TALK ABOUT IT AGAIN ANOTHER TIME?"
(Always finish the conversation with room to pick it back up again later.)

"THANK YOU FOR TELLING ME. "

"I'M SO GLAD YOU ASKED ME."

"HONOR GOD WITH YOUR BODY."

IF YOU EVER FEEL PRESSURED TO DO SOMETHING YOU DON'T WANT TO DO, YOU COULD ALWAYS SAY . . .
(Help them script responses to difficult situations.)

"GUARD YOUR HEART."

"DON'T GIVE SOMEONE CONTROL OF YOUR LIFE."

"WHAT KIND OF FRIEND IS PEYTON?"
(Stay interested in their relationships and ask follow-up questions.)

What do you think about dating in high school? What do you want your ninth grader to know?

_____

_____

_____

_____

_____

_____

_____

_____

_____

_____

_____

_____

_____

_____

_____

_____

_____

_____

_____

_____

_____

_____

What are your views about birth control? If your ninth grader were to ask you about birth control, what would you say?

_____

_____

_____

_____

_____

_____

_____

_____

_____

_____

_____

_____

_____

_____

_____

_____

_____

_____

_____

_____

Over 10% of high schoolers report having been kissed, touched, or physically forced to have intercourse against their will by someone they were dating. How can you guide your ninth grader to know how to get out of potentially dangerous situations?

_____

_____

_____

_____

_____

_____

_____

_____

_____

_____

_____

_____

_____

_____

_____

_____

Plan ahead. Write down two or three things you want to say to your kid if you were to discover something you hadn't expected when it comes to their sexuality. *(It's okay to pray you never have to say these things.)*

_____

_____

_____

_____

_____

_____

_____

_____

_____

_____

_____

_____

_____

_____

_____

_____

_____

_____

Technological responsibility

—

LEVERAGING THE POTENTIAL OF ONLINE EXPERIENCES TO ENHANCE MY OFFLINE COMMUNITY AND SUCCESS

THIS YEAR YOU WILL
EXPAND THEIR POTENTIAL
SO THEY WILL ESTABLISH PERSONAL BOUNDARIES
AND LEVERAGE ONLINE OPPORTUNITIES.

The content your ninth grader posts online may be even more permanent than the permanent record of school grades and disciplinary infractions. Before granting your ninth grader more access, have a few conversations about the platforms they use and how they can be potentially helpful or harmful.

SAY THINGS LIKE . . .

"HOW DO YOU USE SPOTIFY? CAN YOU SET UP A PLAYLIST FOR ME?"
(Know what apps they have and how they use them.)

"HAVE YOU SEEN PEOPLE DO OR SAY THINGS ONLINE THEY WOULD NEVER DO OR SAY IN PERSON? WHY DO YOU THINK THAT HAPPENS?"
(Cue conversations to reflect on how people use digital devices.)

"HOW DO YOU THINK IN-PERSON RELATIONSHIPS ARE AFFECTED BY WHAT PEOPLE SAY ONLINE?"

WHAT YOU POST IS PUBLIC, EVEN IF IT FEELS PRIVATE, AND IT CAN BE PERMANENT.
(Help them recognize potential risks related to the words, images, and videos they create.)

"WHO'S YOUR FAVORITE PERSON TO FOLLOW?"
(Discover who they are listening to online.)

"WHAT ARE SOME FREEDOMS I HAVE ONLINE THAT YOU DON'T HAVE YET?"
(Discuss plans for increasing freedom and responsibility over the next four years.)

What are some ways you've seen your ninth grader use technology to do something good?

_____

_____

_____

_____

_____

_____

_____

_____

_____

_____

_____

_____

_____

_____

_____

_____

_____

_____

_____

What are your concerns about your ninth grader's engagement with digital devices? What rules do you have to help monitor and guard their engagement?

_____

_____

_____

_____

_____

_____

_____

_____

_____

_____

_____

_____

_____

_____

_____

_____

_____

_____

When you aren't sure what to do about an issue related to parenting and technology, who can you go to for advice?

_____

_____

_____

_____

_____

_____

_____

_____

_____

_____

_____

_____

_____

_____

_____

_____

_____

_____

_____

What are your own personal values and disciplines when it comes to leveraging technology? Are there ways you want to improve your own savvy, skill, or responsibility in this area?

_____

_____

_____

_____

_____

_____

_____

_____

_____

_____

_____

_____

_____

_____

_____

_____

_____

Authentic faith

—

TRUSTING JESUS
IN A WAY THAT
TRANSFORMS HOW
I LOVE GOD,
MYSELF,
AND THE REST
OF THE WORLD

THIS YEAR YOU WILL
FUEL PASSION
SO THEY WILL KEEP PURSUING AUTHENTIC FAITH AND DISCOVER A PERSONAL MISSION.

In this phase when your ninth grader is asking, "Where do I belong?" foster their connection to a positive faith community. Your ninth grader will need consistent peers and leaders who will strengthen their relationship with God. So look for ways to prioritize their church connection, and stay engaged in their faith journey by having conversations at home.

SAY THINGS LIKE . . .

"HOW CAN I PRAY FOR YOU TODAY / THIS WEEK?"

"WHEN DO YOU FEEL CLOSEST TO GOD?"

"WHAT'S SOMETHING YOU FEEL LIKE GOD IS TEACHING YOU RIGHT NOW?"

"LATELY, I'M FINDING I CONNECT BEST WITH GOD WHEN I'M . . ."

"THERE'S NOTHING YOU WILL EVER DO THAT COULD MAKE GOD STOP LOVING YOU."

WHEN YOU TOLD ME ABOUT . . . IT MADE ME THINK OF A VERSE IN PROVERBS.
(Share Bible verses that relate to their present circumstances.)

"I DON'T KNOW."

"THAT'S A GOOD QUESTION. I'M NOT SURE I WILL EVER KNOW THE FULL ANSWER, BUT I BELIEVE . . ."
(Let them know it's okay to talk about hard questions.)

What are some ways you can help deepen your ninth grader's connection with friends who follow Jesus?

_____

_____

_____

_____

_____

_____

_____

_____

_____

_____

_____

_____

_____

_____

_____

_____

_____

_____

_____

What are some ways you can help deepen your ninth grader's connection with adults whose faith they admire?

_____

_____

_____

_____

_____

_____

_____

_____

_____

_____

_____

_____

_____

_____

_____

_____

_____

_____

_____

_____

What are some retreats, youth camps, or mission trip opportunities provided by your church or a local youth ministry? Which ones seem most appealing to your ninth grader?

_____

_____

_____

_____

_____

_____

_____

_____

_____

_____

_____

_____

_____

_____

_____

_____

_____

What service opportunities are available for high schoolers at your church? What would it take for you to help them participate?

_____

_____

_____

_____

_____

_____

_____

_____

_____

_____

_____

_____

_____

_____

_____

_____

_____

_____

_____

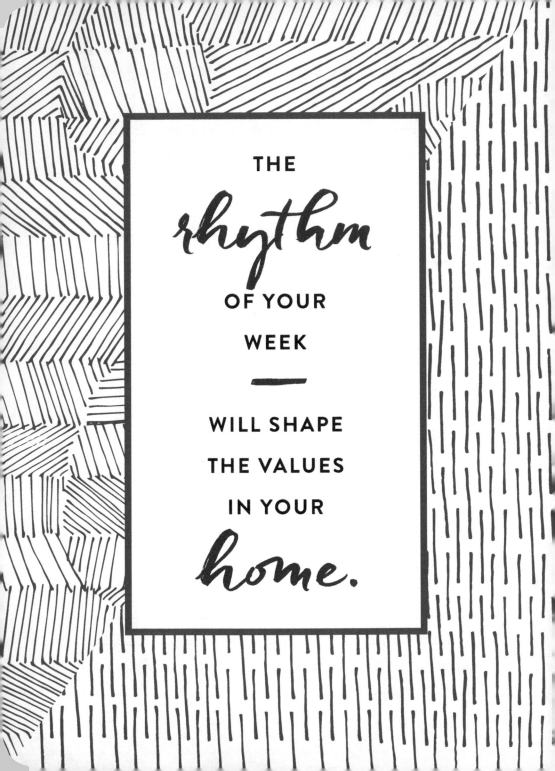

THE

rhythm

OF YOUR

WEEK

—

WILL SHAPE

THE VALUES

IN YOUR

home.

NOW THAT YOU HAVE FILLED THIS BOOK WITH IDEAS, IT MAY SEEM AS IF YOU WILL NEVER HAVE TIME TO GET IT ALL DONE.

Actually, you have *208 weeks.*

And every week has potential.

The secret to making the most of this phase is to find time to spend together—even if it's only a couple hours each week. You may have less quality time together, but look for opportunities during three consistent times (and one that's less predictable).

Instill purpose by starting the day with encouraging words.

Connect regularly by scheduling time to eat together (even if it's once a week).

Interpret life when they occasionally open up at the end of the day. (Stay consistently available—just in case.)

Strengthen your relationship by adjusting your plans to show up whenever they need you.

How are you adjusting to a new rhythm in this phase?

What are some of your favorite traditions with your ninth grader?

_____
_____
_____
_____
_____
_____
_____
_____
_____
_____
_____
_____
_____
_____
_____
_____
_____
_____
_____
_____
_____

Write down any other thoughts or questions that you have about parenting your ninth grader.

_____

_____

_____

_____

_____

_____

_____

_____

_____

_____

_____

_____

_____

_____

_____

_____

_____

TO LOVE GOD

Provoke
discovery

→

SO THEY WILL . . .
TRUST GOD'S CHARACTER
& EXPERIENCE GOD'S FAMILY

 WISDOM
(First day of school)

 FAITH
(Trust Jesus)

AY?

**DO I HAVE YOUR
ATTENTION?**

**DO I HAVE WHAT
IT TAKES?**

**DO I HAVE
FRIENDS?**

K &
FIRST

SECOND
& THIRD

FOURTH
& FIFTH

ENGAGE **their interests**

EVERY KID $\longrightarrow$ MADE I THE IMA OF GO

Incite

wonder $\longrightarrow$ SO THEY WILL . . .
KNOW GOD'S LOVE
& MEET GOD'S FAMILY

BEGINNING
(Baby dedication)

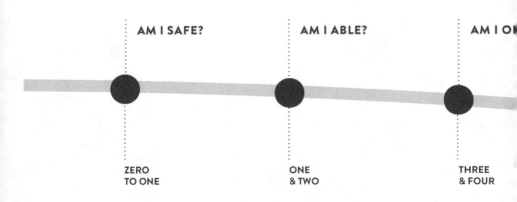

AM I SAFE?　　　AM I ABLE?　　　AM I O

ZERO
TO ONE

ONE
& TWO

THREE
& FOUR

EMBRACE **their physical needs**

YOU HAVE

APPROXIMATELY

208 WEEKS.

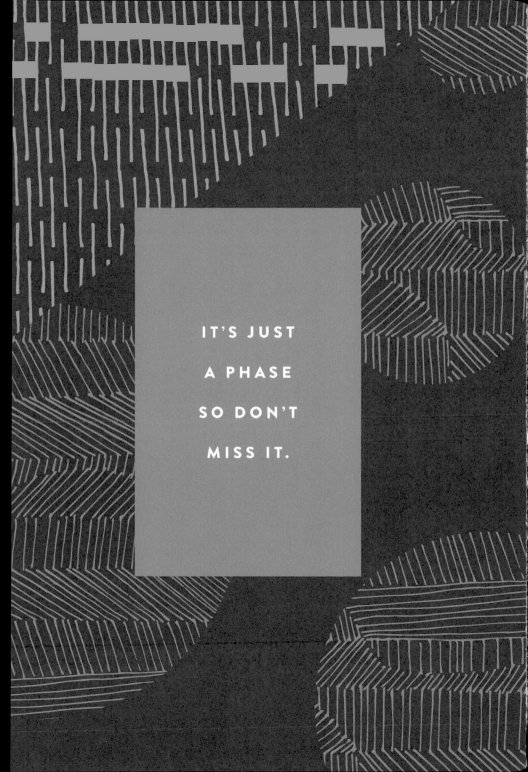

IT'S JUST
A PHASE
SO DON'T
MISS IT.

ND

trust Jesus → **TO HAVE A BETTER FUTURE**

Fuel

passion

→

SO THEY WILL . . .
**KEEP PURSUING AUTHENTIC FAITH
& DISCOVER A PERSONAL MISSION**

 **FREEDOM**
(Driver's license)

 **GRADUATION**
(Moving on)

ERE DO I
ONG?

**WHY
SHOULD I
BELIEVE?**

**HOW CAN I
MATTER?**

**WHAT WILL I
DO?**

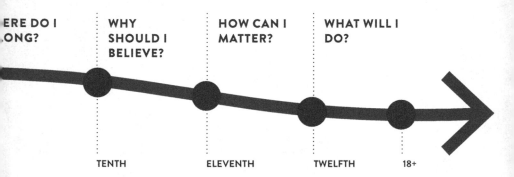

TENTH

ELEVENTH

TWELFTH

18+

MOBILIZE their potential

WITH
ALL THEIR

 HEART

 SOUL

 STRENGTH

A

Provoke

 *discovery*

$\longrightarrow$

SO THEY WILL . . .
OWN THEIR OWN FAITH
& VALUE A FAITH COMMUNITY

 **IDENTITY**
(Coming of age)

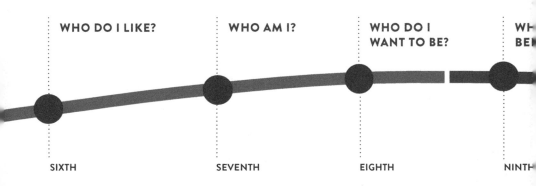

WHO DO I LIKE?	WHO AM I?	WHO DO I WANT TO BE?	WH BE
SIXTH	SEVENTH	EIGHTH	NINTH

AFFIRM their personal journey

PARENTING YOUR NINTH GRADER

ABOUT THE AUTHORS

KRISTEN IVY @kristen_ivy

Kristen Ivy is executive director of the Phase Project. She and her husband, Matt, are in the preschool and elementary phases with three kids: Sawyer, Hensley, and Raleigh.

Kristen earned her Bachelors of Education from Baylor University in 2004 and received a Master of Divinity from Mercer University in 2009. She worked in the public school system as a high school biology and English teacher, where she learned firsthand the importance of influencing the next generation.

Kristen is also the executive director of messaging at Orange and has played an integral role in the development of the elementary, middle school, and high school curriculum and has shared her experiences at speaking events across the country. She is the co-author of *Playing for Keeps, Creating a Lead Small Culture, It's Just a Phase*, and *Don't Miss It*.

REGGIE JOINER @reggiejoiner

Reggie Joiner is founder and CEO of the reThink Group and co-founder of the Phase Project. He and his wife, Debbie, have reared four kids into adulthood. They now also have two grandchildren.

The reThink Group (also known as Orange) is a non-profit organization whose purpose is to influence those who influence the next generation. Orange provides resources and training for churches and organizations that create environments for parents, kids, and teenagers.

Before starting the reThink Group in 2006, Reggie was one of the founders of North Point Community Church. During his 11 years with Andy Stanley, Reggie was the executive director of family ministry, where he developed a new concept for relevant ministry to children, teenagers, and married adults. Reggie has authored and co-authored more than 10 books including: *Think Orange*, *Seven Practices of Effective Ministry*, *Parenting Beyond Your Capacity*, *Playing for Keeps*, *Lead Small*, *Creating a Lead Small Culture*, and his latest, *A New Kind of Leader* and *Don't Miss It*.

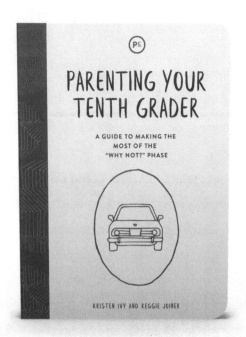

MAKE THE MOST OF EVERY PHASE IN YOUR CHILD'S LIFE

The guide in your hand is one of an eighteen-part series.

So, unless you've figured out a way to freeze time and keep your ninth grader from turning into a tenth grader, you might want to check out the next guide in this set.

Designed in partnership with Parent Cue, each guide will help you rediscover . . .

what's changing about your kid,
the 6 things your kid needs most,
and 4 conversations to have each year.